Basic Property Management

By

Anna Jard

**Diadem Literary Services
Detroit, Michigan**

Basic Property Management

Copyright © 2014 by Antoinette L. Coleman. All rights reserved. No part of this book may be reproduced or transmitted in any form or by any means including graphic, electronic, mechanical, photocopying, recordings, or any information retrieval system without written permission from the publisher, except for brief quotations included in review.

ISBN 978-1-312-67853-8

Published by: Diadem Literary Services, Detroit, Michigan

Printed and bound in the United States of America by Lulu.com.

Contents

	Page
Introduction	5
The History of Real Property	7
What is Property Management?	15
The Tax Credit Program	21
Conventional Properties	25
Subsidy Property	29
Managing a Property	31
Leasing and Property Lease-Ups	49
Laws, Regulation, and Regulating Agencies	55
Competition	61
Waiting Lists	63
Leasing Up a Property	67
The Lease Agreement	69
Resident Retention	83
Attitude and Property Management	89
Handling the 'Hostile' Resident	93
Choosing the 'Right' Employees	99
Managing Stress	105
Handling Emergencies	113

Introduction

The attention of civilization has been placed on the form, placement, and provision of human habitation. The building codes, which specify structural integrity in housing construction are found in the Code of Hammurabi. During the Greek and Roman Empire's City planning activities focused exclusively on the appropriate placement of urban housing from the perspectives of defense and water supply.

As 13th century Europe became a center of trade and commerce, its walls provided a safe haven from nomadic warriors and looters. As the people sheltered themselves within these walls, the demand for urban housing increased. Unplanned additions to and subdivisions of existing structures filled this demand.

Unlike 13th century Europe, ***Basic Property Management*** will instruct the reader on the proper planning of property management. The increased demand for housing can be managed and structured. Move-ins should be complete, and residents should be basically content. Maintenance technicians and Office managers work hand in hand to ensure the satisfaction of the resident and promote the retention of the property conditions according to housing regulations.

Basic Property Management will give the prospective property manager insight into the proper working and maintenance of an apartment community. Where all questions and areas may not be covered, basic property information is offered throughout the book.

We understand that housing is a critical component in the social and economic fabric of all nations. No country, yet, has adequate housing to all the various economic groups that make up its populace. Thus, our regulatory agencies continue to strive in the pursuit of reconditioning our abandoned buildings and properties and promote affordable housing for the low to middle classes of our society. Programs are offered to encourage property owners to build or maintain affordable housing. However, although these problems aren't entirely eradicated, most conditions in the housing problems are being addressed. Where the regulatory agencies stop, **Basic Property Management** begins in assisting these government agencies by giving the insight and instruction associated with property management.

The History of Real Property

The relationship between two parties, the Landlord and the Tenant, which is created by a lease is in the law of real property. The lease is a contract under which the landlord or lessor, who has superior title to the property, grants possession and use of the property to the tenant or lessee. The actual owner doesn't have to be the landlord. The lessee can grant a sublease to another tenant and keep the right to reassume possession of the property either at the end of the specified period or sooner if there is a breach of contract by the lessee.

This contractual relationship originated in the feudal system of land tenure under a system where the superior lord held all freehold land including fees. All landholdings formed a chain of vassalships with ownership descending from the monarch through an overlord to the vassal. The Statute Qula Emptores later abolished this practice in England in 1290. The modern landlord-tenant relationship developed through statutes and laws, judicial decisions, and contractual arrangements.

Estate Laws

Estate, in law, is the degree of interest or ownership a person has in property. The term estate is also to denote the ownership of all property possessed by the individual. Sometimes even the debt of a person is included. The estate or 'the total belongings of a person' is divided into realty (real estate) and personal estate.

Types of Estates

There are two types of estates: freehold and nonfreehold. Freehold estates are the fee simple and the life fee. This is found in modern property law. Fee simple estate is the absolute ownership of land and property, which includes the right to sell or divide property at will. The life fee estate allows the owner to control the land or property during one's lifetime only; the grantor decides who will acquire the property after the death of the life tenant.

Leases of real property establish nonfreehold estates. Two common types are the estate for years and the periodic estate. The former implies the right to occupy the realty for a fixed time; in the latter the lease period is for a definite term that is renewed automatically if neither party signifies an intent to terminate the contract.

Today the term estate refers to property of every sort that is owned and transferred to another at the owner's discretion. A deceased person's estate is disposed of according to law and to instructions given prior to death. An executor is responsible for the disposition of the estate.

Tenure

In the law of real property of feudal England, tenure was the manner in which a person held or owned real property. Under feudalism, the king owned all the land and his vassals (tenants) were entitled to hold portions of the land allotted by the king and under conditions he would impose. The vassals would then divide their lands among others who became vassals.

Housing in the United States

The physical stock of housing in the United States is one of the nation's principal capital assets. About two-thirds of the population live in single-family homes, most of which have been built by small private housing developers who decide which homes the consumers will accept.

Various laws, institutions, and public agencies work to ensure private-market housing is produced safely by builders and delivered efficiently to consumers. Zoning laws control the quantity and the type of housing; the building and housing codes determine the quality of the housing and inclusive services offered. Financing is available from lending institutions whose activities are governed by law. Consumers are afforded access to this housing through a variety of settlement procedures and fair-housing laws.

Types of Housing

Housing in the United States varies significantly in type, age, value, and quality. There are currently, 66 percent single-family homeowners, 10 percent living in two- to four-unit structures, 17 percent in apartment complexes, and the remaining 7 percent in mobile homes.

The quality of American housing is exceptionally high. Less than 2 percent of year-round housing units lack plumbing; about 3 percent have more than 1 person per room; and about 1 percent lack exclusive use of kitchen facilities.

Housing Regulations and Federal Aid

The establishment of housing codes was the earliest public involvement in housing in the United States. The New York Tenement Law of 1867 regulated the physical conditions and maintenance standards of the New York City apartment houses. A few other states soon followed.

The federal government first induced regulating housing when the nations entered World War I in 1917. The event sparked the expansion of defense plants, thus creating a need to house the war workers at particular locations. Congress formed the U.S. Housing Corporation to handle this problem. This corporation remained in existence until the end of the war in 1918.

Property during the Depression Years

During the 1920s, a housing boom occurred in the United States, but it soon plummeted during the Great Depression in the 1930s. The Home Owners' Loan Corporation was a result of this downtime. This corporation was formed to refinance existing home loans. Later, the Federal Housing Administration was authorized in 1934. The FHA insured residential loans, which encouraged lenders to offer long-term (20- or 30-year), fixed-rate mortgages. FHA housing activity received further support when the Federal National Mortgage Association (FNMA) was created in 1938. FNMA, in turn, purchased FHA-insured loans, and established an important secondary market and liquidity (turning real estate into cash) for the local savings and loan associations.

During the 1930s a public housing program was created to clear out the slums and provide low-cost housing for the poor. These programs were implemented by the local housing authorities, which received government assistance. These housing activities stimulated public support systems in the late 1930s, but eventually came to a halt with the advent of World War II (1939-1945).

Housing in the Postwar Era

The federal government in the late 1940s and '50s continued the FHA, the FNMA, and public housing supports. For example, the Veterans' Administration guaranteed loans through a program authorized in 1944. This encouraged the development of the postwar suburban land subdivisions.

The Housing Act of 1949 authorized the 'urban renewal' of slum areas. This was the most significant program and strategy in the postwar era. Under this act, deteriorated properties were demolished. Then the cleared tracts were sold to private developers for a nominal sum. The main focus of this program was to eliminate slums and build new residential and nonresidential units. However, this program came under criticism with the over-emphasized demolition and the detriment of viable neighborhoods and poor or minority residents.

In the 1960s, the federal government changed its housing involvement from demolition to rehabilitation of housing. In addition, new and expanded subsidies were provided for poor and minority households. The Housing Act of 1965 created the program that made subsidies available for low- and moderate-income rental units and foster home ownership by the poor. The best-known subsidy plan was the Model Cities Program, which was authorized by the 1966 Demonstration Cities Act. It focused on upgrading the physical housing and public facilities as well as the social aspects of the inner city.

In 1965, A cabinet-level agency formed was the Department of Housing and Urban Development. HUD was in charge of aiding new towns, self-contained communities, and incorporated integrating residential and nonresidential uses.

The 1970s and 1980s

By the 1970s and 1980s, problems emerged in the existing housing programs. Their new owners abandoned single-family homes bought by the poor increasingly. Several of the privately developed and assisted new towns experienced bankruptcy. These conditions evoked a moratorium and caused a redirection of approaches to housing problems. Block grants were then created through the Community Development Block Grant program, authorized by the Housing Act of 1978. The CDBG program, was more broad-based by allowing flexibility in local housing problems. It provided 'blocks' of money for urban revitalization. The allocation of block grants was a primary redevelopment approach in the 1980s, although funding for CDBG and other programs was reduced.

Further changes in focus went from rebuilding the direst neighborhoods to improving the 'gray' areas that were beginning to decline. The government realized that it was more cost effective to rehabilitate and preserve existing housing structures. So, HUD ordered a stop to the construction of new housing developments. Many cities and private ventures were encouraged to renovate brownstones and row houses, but these actions didn't help the poor people. So, the housing shortage worsened.

Racial Discrimination

The Fair Housing Act was passed by Congress in 1968, which barred racial discrimination in the sale, rental, or financing of housing where federal monies were involved by way of loans, mortgages, or grants. The U.S. attorneys were authorized to sue any noncomplying state agencies. Similarly, the Equal Employment Opportunity Commission, established in 1964, was authorized to file suit as well.

What is Property Management?

Property Management is the management of a housing community as outlined by the governmental rules and regulations handed down through the federal regulatory agencies. Property management isn't as easy as running a business. In order to be successful at maintaining a property, there must be a great amount of dedication and concern for the property and its residents. Without this dedication, the property can become unpleasant and unprofitable for both the residents and the property owners. This is why there has to be a specific handpicked staff for each type of property in order for it to succeed.

Types of Properties

There are different types of properties and each type is slightly different from the other. A few types are Conventional, Senior Citizen Tax Credit, and Subsidized.

The Conventional is one of the easiest to rent because limited criteria are needed to approve the prospective resident. Usually just identification, employment check stubs or a letter from an employer, a previous landlord letter, and a credit report are required to approve or decline an applicant residency in the community.

The Tax Credit property focuses mainly on income qualifications, which is regulated by income guidelines for each region where there is a tax credit property. The applicants usually consist of young people who are out on their own for the first time, small families just starting out and retired workers. Seldom will there be established families looking for an apartment or qualifying for an apartment in this community.

Many times, the Tax Credit community is mistaken for subsidized property because of the low-income base, but the difference is apparent. The Tax Credit property qualifies the applicants' income. This program will have income parameters set forth by the Michigan State Housing and Development Association. So, if an applicant's income is below or above these set standards, they will not qualify.

The Subsidized property unlike Tax Credit properties will 'tailor fit' your rent to meet your household income. The Housing Commissions servicing the properties in their district or county usually pay the difference directly to the properties. A monthly report and a yearly qualification process have to be followed in order to keep these government monies.

Subsidized properties have income limits that help the apartment management staff determine if the applicant qualifies for the assistance or not. Some properties will only allow qualified applicants to acquire an apartment in the apartment community. Then, there are other communities, which will allow any and all applicants who are low-income or otherwise to acquire an apartment in their communities.

In any wise, these properties are run in some ways similar to the Tax Credit properties in that they both have government income guidelines and require yearly recertification for government-assisted monies.

Manpower Required

Property management not only depends on the type of property being managed, but a specialized dedicated staff to manage. Dependent on the type of property, the staff can make the difference between a successful property and a failing one. For example, a Senior Citizen property might require a management team that is very patience, understanding, and compassionate. Because this community consists of seniors who have spent their lives helping to build our society, a little consideration and understanding would benefit the residents as well as the staff.

I heard it once said that; "A good property has a good working team!" If everyone isn't working for the sake of a good managed property, then there will be problems with resident retention, property maintenance, and staff dedication. If there is one 'bad apple' in the bunch, the other employees may become discouraged. It is most important to employ people who care for the betterment of the property and its residents. Sometimes this can be a trial and error basis.

Last, a pleasant disposition between the office staff and the maintenance staff has to be maintained. It is the responsibilities of the property manager to promote this type of working atmosphere by displaying this attitude. When perspective renters enter the office, and see the unity and joy displayed between the staff, it can change their attitude towards the property. Even residents who see and have experienced the unity of the office staff tend to have confidence in the completion of necessary requests they submit.

Attitude plays a big part in the success of a property and shouldn't be taken lightly. In my own experiences, when I went apartment shopping I was deterred from renting at an apartment complex because of the attitude of the office personnel. In other cases, because of the pleasant attitude of the office staff, I was glad to rent the apartment. I trusted that they were excited about their product because it was a good product.

Curb Appeal

The outward appearance of a property; neatly cut lawns, flowers, clean building interiors and exteriors, etc. can make the difference between a successful and an unsuccessful rental. Good Curb Appeal can help drawn in passers by who may recommend your property just from its appearance.

Good Curb Appeal tells the apartment shopper how much you care about your residents and the property. It can also promote business for other apartment communities within the Management Company. Curb Appeal promotes good reputation and business that the property would not usually receive. Last, it reflects the type of maintenance team the property management company has working for it.

Rules and Regulations

Another area that can promote the success of a property is the maintenance of the rules and regulations of the Housing Authorities, the Management Company, and the property rental agreement. Without the enforcing of these rules, there cannot be unity and safety in the apartment community. One rule my regional manager encouraged me with that helped me in my apartment management career was, "Never let the resident get comfortable with not following the rules of their contact." This is where the hard work comes in, believe it or not.

Walking the property and actually listening to the complaints of your residents are important. Most importantly acting on them immediately. Making sure the entire property understands the restrictions of the property.

The manager should send notices with information about the property and new regulations that may have been decided on as a result of unforeseen events that occurred on the property. All these things take a lot of hard work, dedication, and attention. If a property manager gets lazy in handling these duties, then the property can easily slip into non-compliance to these rules and regulations.

A lot of these rules and regulations are government regulated and most be upheld by the property management and its residents. Sometimes broken government rules can cost the management company and the ownership lots of monies. In some cases, it could cost the loss of the apartment licenses and certificates. So, this can be the breaking or making of a good property.

Conclusion

We talked over a few areas of property management, but these areas are what property management is all about. When all the required areas are performed and upheld with the highest of dedication from its employees, then the property will profit and the ownership will also. Property management is the production of people renting a product for profiting of the ownership and the supplying of a need for shelter to the renter.

The Tax Credit Program

One of the most popular low- to moderate-income housing programs today is the Tax Credit Housing Program. This program operates under Section 42 of the Internal Revenue Code of 1986 and refers to the low- to moderate-income requirements that the resident has to qualify into in order to acquire an apartment under this program.

Application Process

The applicant has to fill out the application fully, making sure to answer every question. Then a checklist is filled out outlining every kind of income a person could possibly have. The checklist should reflect the information on the application and likewise.

Next, verification forms are sent out to every source of income with a 'yes' answer. These verification forms can be mailed, and some can be mailed and faxed over. The applicant is not permitted to 'take' any verification forms with them and they are not permitted to submit anything from their sources of income.

If there is a problem in obtaining any income information, at that point in time and after every effort on the part of management's part to obtain the information has been exhausted, the applicant can submit at least 6 check stubs from the most recent back, 6 bank statements from the most recent back, or any other income information that is in hard copy.

All verifications have to be within a 60-day period and no longer than 90 days. If the information is older than 90 days, then more recent information has to be obtained before the applicant can qualify for the Tax Credit Program.

Income Certification

The Department of Housing and Urban Development sends out an income qualification listing every year with new income limitations and rent limitations to the property ownerships that are under the Tax Credit Program. The properties use these criteria in the selecting of qualified applicants in the low- to moderate-income classification. The listing goes according to a percentage of the national average income per family size. These percentages could be from 30% of the national average income per family size to 60% of the average income per family size.

Each year the residents have to re-qualify their yearly income to a limit of 140% of the new HUD income limitations. The resident is responsible for submitting all pertinent information required to recertify their household to remain for the Tax Credit property.

If at the time of recertification, the resident's income exceeds the 140% income increase they are allotted, they can still remain on the property as long as the next similar unit is rented at the rental percentage as this particular resident's unit.

Students

A qualifying family has to have at least one member of the family who is not a student. It can be an infant, but at least one member cannot be attending school.

If a student does apply, then they will not qualify because the government has already provided housing for them through the Universities and Colleges. Thus, the Tax Credit Program will not qualify students.

Rents

As with any property, by law there must be a 30-day notice if a change in rent or in any previous contractual agreement. In the Tax Credit Program, the rent cannot exceed the total suggested rents HUD has set forth. This rent includes the residents' monthly utility payments. Thus, if the suggested rent is $900.00 and the utility allowance is $60.00 dollars, the highest rent that can be set is $840.00. Rents set at a rent less than the suggested rent as well.

Certain Changes

The resident has to notify the manager of any changes in the following areas: household size, income, job changes, and student status. These areas can affect whether the family will still qualify for the program.

Outside of these above-mentioned qualifications, the rules and regulations of the Tax Credit run property are the same as any other property.

Conventional Properties

I feel the easiest property to run paper wise is a conventional property. Conventional Properties are usually occupied by working class people who either have incomes through jobs, social security and pensions, or through their own businesses. Because there usually aren't any government-assisted programs run through Conventional Properties, qualifying residents are easier and not as time consuming.

Application Process

The applicant can fill out an applicant and later submit a letter of employment outlining their years of service, date of hire, yearly, monthly, or hourly pay rate, social security number, and home address. Then, a landlord reference can be submitted to determine if they were good residents at their present address. Last, a credit report can be pulled. There is no income limitation other than the 3 times the rent rule.

Qualifying Income

The 3 times the rent rule says that the prospective resident has to make 3 times the monthly rent times twelve. For example, it the rental amount per month in an apartment complex is $600.00, then the calculation would be as follows:

600 X 3 X 12 = $21,600

So, if an applicant is applying for an apartment renting for $600 per month, his/her income has to be $21,600 or greater. This rule is prevalent across the broad for most properties. Some properties use 2 ½ times the rent, but most will use the 3 times the rent rule.

Tax Credit properties will use this rule but will have an income ceiling handed down through HUD. If an income limit for a two-family household is $21,600 and the monthly rent is $500 per month for the apartment, then the two-family household could have to have an income between $18,000 and $21,600. If this household's income falls below or exceeds these parameters, they will not qualify for the property.

Another difference in income qualifications between the conventional and tax credit properties is that an applicant cannot pay more than 35 to 40 percent of their income into rents and utilities. The conventional property suggests that if the income is above the recommended low, then they can afford the rent. There is a ratio that can be followed. Usually, the ratio of expenses against available income can determine if an applicant qualifies for a conventional property.

Lease Renewal

Unlike the Tax Credit property, when a resident's lease is up for renewal, the management office has to just type up the new lease and sent out notification for scheduling the resident's signing.

As stated in the section for Tax Credit recertification, all new and pertinent income information has to be obtained and calculated before a resident's lease can be renewed.

Lease Terminations

When a resident comes to the end of his/her contract and he/he chooses to vacant at the time of lease expiration, a 30-day notice to move has to be submitted by the resident to management 30 days before the lease expires. If the 30-day notice is sent in the middle of the lease term, there is usually a termination fee and possibly other fees charged before the lease can be terminated. This practice is usually the standard for most types of properties.

Subsidy Property

Unlike the Conventional and Tax Credit properties, the Subsidy property will calculate what rents are afforded to the resident while the Federal Housing Agencies will pay the different.

Applications

The application process is similar to the Tax Credit application. All income is verified through third party form verifications. The only difference is that in the subsidy program, expenses are also counted in the determination of affordable monthly rents. A few of those expenses accounted for are childcare, medical bills and prescriptions, along with other expenses.

Qualifying Criteria

There are qualifying criteria for qualifying for the subsidy program. A qualifying household has to have 30 percent or less of the national average income per family size. If the applicant or resident exceeds this limitation, they will lose their subsidy and be required to pay the full amount of monthly rent or be required to move.

Lease Renewals

As income and household information change, the subsidy monthly rent amount will change. The information reporting process can be more frequent than on any other housing assisted property. So, leases can change 2 or more times during the course of the year. Of course, the actually yearly lease renewal would still occur around the anniversary date that the resident moved into the community.

Property Similarities

The lease, amenities, etc. are usually the same for most apartment communities. The only differences are in the qualifying criteria and application processes, which vary according to the property programs.

Managing a Property

A property manager has a great responsibility in upholding the rules and regulations of the Government Housing Authorities as well as enforcing the terms of the rental agreement and/or contracts between the resident and the owner. Additional responsibilities of a property manager are processing accounting and monthly budget reports, delegating responsibilities, decision making, staff reviews, rent collections and delinquencies, handling court issues, skip outs, advertising, and resident programs, with a host of other duties that may arise.

Accounting and Monthly Budgets

Documents that provide systematic information about financial affairs of a business or institution are called Financial Reports and Statements. Accountants usually prepare these reports. The manager usually performs bookkeeping duties.

History of Bookkeeping

Bookkeeping and record-keeping methods were created when trade and commerce were on the rise and were preserved from ancient and medieval sources. Double-entry bookkeeping began in medieval Italy and was well developed in Genoa from 1340. Luca Pacioli wrote the first published accounting work, which have remained essentially unchanged. These works included early formulations of the assets, liabilities, and income concepts and were additionally published in Italian, German, Dutch, French, and English during the 16th century.

By the 19th century, the role of accounting and bookkeeping was redefined with the industrial Revolution. These accounting techniques had to be adequate in handling the mechanization, factory-manufacturing operations of publicly held business corporations, which were owned by absentee stockholders and administrated by professional managers.

Classifications for Accounting

There are two categories for accounting information: financial accounting or public information and managerial accounting or private information. Financial accounting pertains to the financial position, the liquidity (that is, the ability to convert to cash), and the profitability of an enterprise or corporation. This information usually is submitted to stockholders, creditors, customers, suppliers, regulatory commissions, financial analysts, and trade associations.

Managerial accounting usually isn't disseminated outside of the company. It deals with cost-profit-volume relationships, planning and control, efficiency and productivity, capital budgeting, pricing decisions, and any other relative matters. Primarily division managers, department heads use this information, along with project directors, section supervisors, and other managers.

The Principle behind Financial Reporting

The purpose behind financial reports is to document how effectively the managers manage the owners' assets, in terms of capital preservation and profit generation.

Only recent accounting principles are prescribed in statutory law. The systematic compiling and recording of financial transactions include invoices, payroll time cards, bank checks, and receiving reports. The 'keeping' of a sales journal, a purchase journal, a cash-receipts journal, and a cash-disbursements journal are used to record recurring transactions. This practice is most commonly used in property management.

Property Management and Bookkeeping

It is important to keep track of the monthly budget. There are daily reports such as cash receipts journals for rents, deposit slips for the depositing of cash receipts, and a rent roll of outstanding rents owed which are kept. These reports help the manager keep track of the flow of revenue through the property daily and weekly. These reports also inform the Management Company on the day-to-day progress of rent revenues in order to commit to their cash disbursement responsibilities.

Every year the Managing Company sends a budget of scheduled spending and maintaining to the property managers. The manager shouldn't spend more than 75% of the allotted monies for each item listed in the budget. For example, if the property is allowed to spend $300.00 in office supplies, you are actually allowed to spend $225.00. The reasoning behind this procedure is during the month-to-month operations of a property, sometimes unexpected expenses arise that are not included in the budget. To ensure that there isn't a large loss to income, this practice of spending only 75% of the allotted cash is followed. This method creates the availability of existing monies to cover unexpected expenses.

The manager should also keep an open line of communication with the staff on the purchasing and the use of materials. A balance sheet with previous monthly expenditures and present projected allowances should be presented in a monthly staff meeting. This will involve everyone in the task of keeping spending down. Also, it will give everyone a sense of participation in managing property monies.

Monthly ledger reports and quarterly ledger reports should always be referred to and brought to the attention of all employees for the promotion of property progress. The whole staff is responsible for the success of the property financially as well as physically. Thus, showing the monetary progress of the property ensures the employees of job security on that property and will boost their morale through a feeling of always knowing how the property is doing financially.

The Accounting Executive

Some companies refer to their area managers as Regional Managers while others refer to them as Accounting Executives. It is important for the property manager to keep good communication skills with the Accounting Executive. If any problems arise that involve the Housing Regulatory Commissions, it is the job of the Accounting Executive to inform the manager as to how the situation can be handled without violating any of the housing regulations.

The Accounting Executive is the 'guru' of housing laws and regulations. The knowledge of housing resources and agencies are in the hands of the Accounting Executive. The prosperity of the property is not only the responsibility of the property staff but the Accounting Executive. They are the analysts of the apartment market community. They are the eyes and ears of the business. They are also the moneymakers of the management organization.

Contracts and Agreements

Another responsibility of the manager is the enforcing of all contracts and agreements made between the property, the residents, and the outside contractors. At the time a resident move into the apartment community, in most cases, the manager is the person reviewing the contract with the resident. Having a manager explain the rules and regulations of the community can be more forceful to the resident than a rental consultant.

A good property manager will know the rules and regulations of the rental agreement to the extent that if anyone is in violation, the person is notified to comply or suffer cost for the violation or worse, have their contract terminated.

The manager should know residents on the property in order to deal with them. When I managed a Tax Credit property, I went jogging with one resident while discussing the benefits of keeping her rental agreement in tact to term. It worked! She thought I was a nut, but she admired my persistence in keeping her a resident for the remaining months of the year. Get

Managing a Property

to know your residents. Meet with the prospective resident each time they enter the office. It's surprising how much you learn about people in a few short discussions.

Anything the contract states concerning the abilities of the property and the promised 'extras' maintain. Encourage the whole staff to adhere to the conditions of the contract without partiality.

Sometimes, staff members can befriend residents. This is okay as long as there is no partiality shown between residents. This can be a violation of contract and can cause job losses. Encourage the importance of adhering to the contract. All staff members should know the contract as well as the office staff.

Keep a routine of what is recommended in the contract. Keep the residents aware that although they are renting, there is still a contractual obligation. They must abide by the rules they agreed to at the time of their signing. When notifying a resident of a contractual violation, always bring to their attention that this was what they agreed to when they signed their contract.

The manager must keep the apartment community in agreement with the contract in order for the property to prosper in resident retention. There may be disagreements between residents and a difference of opinion between residents and staff, but if the contract is upheld without partiality between the residents and the managing staff, these things are minor. The property morale will remain intact. Guaranteed!

Delegation of Responsibilities

The daily tasks of a manager can become bothersome and hectic if there isn't some type of structure or organization. Sometimes, the manager may have to delegate some managerial responsibilities to the rest of the staff. The one thing that can cripple a business is having a staff that has lack of training in everyday tasks. Everyone from the maintenance employees to the office employees should be cross-trained in basic daily tasks. All employees should know how to answer phones or show apartments.

In the apartment business community, there are no big and little people. Everyone should know how to entreat anyone who enters the property. Prospective residents will sometimes approach a maintenance tech just to see what response they receive. If the technician is professional enough, the shopper will be directed to the office or offered business hour information. Sales should not be attempted by anyone but the leasing consultant.

The staff should be well versed in what their responsibilities are and to what extent they are allowed to promote the property. The manager should learn the abilities of each staff member to ensure that they are used to their greatest potential. There is occasion that a maintenance technician can be most influential in renting apartments. Some maintenance technicians have such personal appeal that their charm alone can influence a potential rental to select your community from which to rent an apartment.

Cross training in some cases, can be the worst thing you can do with some staff members. They may not possess the caliper to perform any other task than the one they were hired to do. Once again, it is vital that the manager learns the abilities of each staff member.

Skip Outs

Sometimes, when a resident realizes they can no longer afford the rent, rather than wait until their contract expires, they will move out of their apartment without notifying the Management Company. This is referred to as a 'skip out' or a 'skip.'

When a manager finds that the previous resident has left an apartment vacant without notice to the rental office, the same court procedures used to evict a resident has to be followed. The reason for this is as long as the contract is intact between the property and the resident; the resident is still responsible for the apartment. After proper procedures have been met. There would be no need for the bailiff to come out. The manager can just take procession of the apartment.

Making Decisions

The corporation members and the accounting executives the majority of the time will not reside on the property. Thus, their eyes and ears will be the property managers. Major decisions that the corporation or the accounting executives make are based on the property information the manager submits to them on a weekly, monthly, and yearly basis. That is why managers need to be very specific and precise in their observations and conclusions.

Property incomes specs can make the difference between whether rent increases will occur for the property or a property rental freeze. On Tax Credit properties, the rent should seldom go up for the residents, but new resident criteria should promote higher rents because of the rise in the income limitations.

It is important that all vital and important information is updated by the manager and submitted to all company parties involved.

The manager is responsible for basic decisions for the property. Those decisions include when yearly preventative maintenance is scheduled, whether or not a resident is charged for repairs as a result of their neglect, and other issues that are contractual. Decisions on staff time off, etc. is left up to the property manager. Major monetary decisions are usually the responsibility of the accounting executive: however, if in question about any decisions, the accounting executive can steer the manager in the right direction.

Staff Reviews

Around review time, the Management Company will send paperwork for each employee. It is the responsibility of the manager to give each employee a written review. In my own experiences, a good manager will always keep a log of each employee's extra achievement or special task. Employee suggestions should always be put in writing and submitted to the main office for evaluation or approval. A copy should be kept in the employee's file. When review time comes, a copy of the written suggestions and special tasks the employee performed throughout the year is attached to the review. This validates the assertiveness of the employee and the dedication displayed throughout the year. Following this procedure will also ensure that the employee is worthy of the manager's recommended merit raise.

The manager should also meet with each employee as to the goals set for the next year to improve performance of the employee or the improvement property conditions. These are the elements of improvement Management Companies usually include in their review of the managing property. They want to know that their managing staff is knowledgeable of all the needs of their properties and are seeking methods of meeting those needs, economically.

Last, the employee evaluation allows the employee to see how much growth has occurred in the job position or how much growth is required for the job position. It informs the manager of the required training each staff member might require meeting the goals set for the improvement of property management.

Rent Collections and Delinquencies

Every property has a cut off for rental payments before it is considered late. Usually this guideline is handed down from the main office to all properties across the board so that there is a uniform method of collecting rents. However, properties have unsaid policies that can most times cause a problem. When collecting rents, abide by the rules and guidelines the contract related to the resident. If the contractual rental terms are enforced from the beginning and maintained, then there should be little problem in collecting rents. If the rules are bent even for a short time, then a new guideline can develop and roam free throughout your property with little assistance from the manager.

If a resident is delinquent with rental payments, follow the contract to the letter. Unfortunately, the resident may become an example to other renters to deter further delinquencies from developing. Above all always remember to never be partial to anyone. Entreat every resident the same. The contract was formed to be a uniform method of managing the property without question. It should be adhered to without question. But, if an occasion should arise that a situation is not outlined in the contract or a rule of the contract is unclear, consult the accounting executive.

Court and Rent Delinquencies

The contract will outline what day in the month a rental payment is considered late. A standard late fee is charged, and a notice sent allowing the resident another 7-day period to submit their full monthly rental payment or release the apartment back into the hands of the property manager.

After the 7-day period is fulfilled and payment or the apartment is not submitted to the manager, the 7-day notice is sent to the property attorney along with the rental contract and any other documents. The attorney processes this document for court and a court case is established. The manager is notified as to the date and time the delinquency cases will be reviewed by the court system. In most cases, the manager has to attend with the attorney in order to answer any questions that may arise.

The resident is also notified via the mail system of the impending court hearing if payment isn't submitted to the management office. It is the manager's responsibility to find out the problem around the delinquent rent. If it is due to a negligent maintenance problem, then it should be resolved before the court hearing. If not resolved, it could cost the property the unpaid rent plus other costs. If resolved, a minimal cost could still be incurred to the property. This should institute a method of ensuring that all delinquency issues aren't maintenance related.

If the delinquency has only to do with a lack of financial resources on the part of the resident, the manager should consult the accounting executive as to what resolutions are available to the resident without compromising the integrity of the rental agreement between the resident and the property. When you meet with the attorney, the manager and the Management Company should be in agreement as to what will transpire between the resident and the property.

All agreements should be in writing. Any arrangements, the attorney will have in writing after an arrangement is arrived at the time of the court hearing. However, it is still good to have your own documentation ready. The whole purpose is to make this transition as uneventful as possible.

If all arrangements are not met within the agreed time frame allotted the resident, then the courts are notified, and a writ is issued for the removal of the resident from the property. The bailiff is then called by the attorneys after the judge signs the writ and returns it to the attorneys' office. The manager is always notified of the status of the writ, etc.

The bailiff will come out to the property and hand the resident notice to move or be evicted from off the premises. Usually 48 hours is given to the residents to remove all personal articles from the residency. After the 48 hours, the bailiff will contact the manager to see if the resident has moved. The manager can send a property agent to check the residency if keys have not been turned into the office. But, the agent cannot enter the premises unless the bailiff is present.

Most times, the resident will have moved, but if not, the bailiff will set up a day with the manager when he/she will come out. A property representative has to be present for the bailiff. The manager can accompany the bailiff in case the resident chooses to pay the account in full at that time. If arrangements have been made by the resident and accepted by the Management Company and the manager, then it would be more important for the manager to accompany the bailiff, at least if there is a paying resident.

Advertising

As the leasing consultant receives and processes applications for residency, the prospective resident will indicate what promotion directed them to the property. This is vital as to what advertisement is most effective in drawing prospective rentals. The manager can decide if a certain circular is ineffective in promoting rentals and discontinue subscription. This would reduce cost to property without change in the rental promotion market. In any wise, the manager should always keep track of what means of advertisement is effective in promoting the property.

Resident Programs

Part of resident retention is resident programming. A good manager will know the needs of the property and provide for them. Also, part of that need is offering different activities to the community. During the holidays, decorating contests could be run along with festive parties to show the holiday aspects of the Management Company. Prizes can consist of useful things like rent reductions or just evenings out to a popular restaurant.

Other ways of showing the residents that the Management Company appreciates their residency is making help information for different organizations in the area available. A good manager knows when a resident is having problems and will attempt to offer any help to resolve those problems. Information is the best help to offer a person in need. It will help promote a community that is caring and heart-filled.

Good grounds and apartment maintenance is the overall method for good resident retention. Having beautification periods for the residents and offering to purchase the flowers or shrubs can promote a closer community. We had a flower-planting day where everyone who wanted to plant flowers were out planting including me. I planted the main drive and as my residents drove by, they were so tickled to see the manager down in the soil planting flowers.

Resident parties, bar-be-ques, etc. are good forms of promoting resident retention, but a sincere love for the residents and a desire to maintain good living conditions will always rank far above any other methods named above or otherwise.

Resident and Management Staff Relations

Property management is a business that can get away from you very easily through the relationships between the resident and the management staff. The management staff should always deal with residents from a professional disposition. If there are any discrepancies in the way resident concerns are addressed, the manager should be the one to whom these concerns are submitted.

Maintenance technicians should not hold conferences with the residents to address any grievances, concerns, disagreements, etc. that the residents may have with the manager. There must always be projected a sense of unity amongst the property management personal. If the manager happens to make a bad decision call on a situation, any disagreements between the staff members must remain between the staff members.

Remember, if the residents feel there is no unity between the manager and the staff, they will have little confidence in the staff's ability to work toward the common goal of property management. Project unity to ensure resident harmony.

Leasing and Property Lease-ups

Leasing is one of the most important aspects of Property Management. It assures that as vacant apartments come available there are prospective applicants at hand to fill those vacancies. When reviewing applicants for occupancy, there is a number of qualifying criteria that should be considered; that is, applications, credit reports, bodies per bedroom, laws and regulations, regulating agencies, competition, waiting lists and apartment availability.

The Application

The most important form in the renting market is the application. It contains all the information pertinent to the leasing process. The required personal information about the applicant should be listed on the application. All areas of the application should be filled. All questions should be answered. If there is a question that is not relevant to the applicant, a 'n/a' or a line should be written in that area. This would inform the rental consultant that the applicant did attempt to answer the question.

All questions should be answered with some degree of certainty and precision. If there are unclear answers, these should be address immediately. Sometimes the applicant may not understand the question. Go over the application with the applicant before the applicant is filled out.

In the Tax Credit application process, the applicant has to be complete. There cannot be any unanswered questions or approximated income figures stated on the application. Everything has to be cut and dry. In my own opinion, all applications should be answered with conclusive answers. There shouldn't be any approximations, especially when income is involved. The average worker knows their yearly income.

When the information is confirmed, the application and the confirmation forms should line up. For example, if an applicant states that their income is $30,000 per year, the employer should also state on the verification form a figure close to or around that $30,000. There was a case in my own experience where a truck driver states he made $29,000 per year and his employee sent back the verification form stating $40,000 per year. Of course, this was a problem. The property the truck driver was applying for was a Tax Credit property, so there were income limitations this amount would have exceeded. Procedural wise, the truck driver should have been declined, but because I knew truck drivers and their income, I checked again with verified check studs from the driver for the last six months and asked the employee to further explain his submission.

The verification of information on the application should be as close as possible. If the information in the above stated paragraph had been true, there would not have been any further investigation. A letter of declination would have been sent and the application with it verification forms would have been filed. It is imperative to store away declined application for a span of 2 years. In case the property is audited, there would be proof that all types of people were given the chance to apply for residency during the leasing process.

Credit Reports

Another aspect of background checking is the credit report. The credit report gives the credit history of the applicant. It tells what type of financial state the applicant has. This information can be reviewed to determine if the applicant has too much responsibility to handle the monthly rental payments or if they would be on time with their payments. Sometimes, the applicant can be someone who only pays their rent on time and let all other bills can go lacking.

When in doubt, a landlord reference can be obtained to determine further if the applicant would be a good candidate for residency. The landlord reference should be obtained in any case.

Credit reports can also be obtained along with background checks. It would depend on the Credit Company that the Management Company deals with.

There is a scoring system that most credit reports have. Most people with good credit will have a score of 600 or better. Sometimes a score of 503 can be good if present credit payments are on time. If a credit reports reflects 'on-time' payments more frequently than late payments, the prospective rent could be considered. If the credit report reflects an even amount of 'on-time' payments and late payments, then it would be at the discretion of the manager or the accounting executive to permit residency of the applicant.

In any wise, the credit report will tell the story of how well an applicant pays bills and if paying obligations are important to the applicant. In some situations, this might not be the case. Unusual situations or unhappy situations may cause problems with the applicant's credit report. So, there are cases where written explanations can clarify the circumstances behind the condition of the applicant's credit report. Again, in any case, it would be at the discretion of the manager to decide whether to accept the application or decline it on the basis of the credit report.

Bodies per Bedroom

Believe it or not, most cities have ordinances that govern how many people can occupy a bedroom or an apartment. The determining factors can depend on the size of the apartment. But, the overall rule is two people per bedroom. The rule is to assure there is not over crowding of living area space per square mile. The apartment community can sometimes create a problem with this ordinance if not regulated. Thus, when in doubt, two people per bedroom should be enforceable.

Laws, Regulations, and Regulating Agencies

The Department of Housing and Urban Development known as HUD and the Michigan State Housing Development Authority along with other agencies have developed and will enforce housing laws and regulations of which all Property Management Companies have to comply. These agencies ensure that the renter will be offered the most affordable and proficient living conditions according to the guidelines set up by the local, state, and government laws.

HUD is a part of the executive branch of the United States government and is responsible for promoting the improvement and development of urban areas. Congress created this department in 1965. A secretary who is appointed by the president with the approval of the Senate and who is a member of the cabinet administers HUD.

HUD carries out research in public housing improvements, housing finance issues, and proposed tax changes. It provides aid to neighborhood rehabilitation projects and anti-discrimination in housing activities. It absorbed the programs in public housing of the old Housing and Home Finance Agency, as well as the mortgage insurance programs of the Federal Housing Administration. In addition, it assumed responsibility for the new programs launched under the Housing and Urban Development Act of 1965. This included the rent-supplements program, which encouraged private enterprise to construct affordable and desirable housing for low-income families.

At present the functions of HUD may be grouped into six major housing categories, which are:

1. Facilitating the production of new and rehabilitated housing;
2. Conserving and preserving existing housing;
3. Insuring mortgages for single-family and multifamily housing along with home improvement loans;
4. Providing housing subsidies for low- and moderate-income housing;
5. Making direct loans to construct or rehabilitate housing projects for the elderly and disabled;
6. Loans for the purchase of manufactured (mobile) homes.

Fair Housing Training

The Fair Housing and Equal Opportunity programs oversee polices that affect civil rights in housing and community development. The accounting

Laws, Regulations, and Regulatory Agencies

executives usually have contacts within the different government agencies that they work hand and hand with. Thus, their knowledge and affiliations makes them the most valuable people in the Management Community. Whatever training is required for the management staff, the accounting executive can obtain information for enrollment.

It would be to the best interest of the manager and the managing staff to attend whatever classes the Fair Housing and Equal Opportunity programs offer to ensure none of the regulatory laws is broken. These classes can help ensure all employees are careful when dealing with prospective renters and residents.

Occasionally, the commissions and apartment rental organizations will send out people to 'shop' properties then report back to the Management Companies with the results on the proficiency of their 'shopped' properties. This allows the Management Company to see how well the manager has trained the property employees and how well the property is being managed.

Listed below are a few conditions that should be avoided when renting to prospective residents:

1. Never give out information as to the ethnic backgrounds of the residents or the nationality, ethnic percentages of the property. This would promote a form of discrimination and the participation of discrimination

2. between the applicant and the management employees.
3. Never make statements about the appearance of the applicant. For example, a woman can look pregnant and not be pregnant. Allow the applicant to mention if there is a baby expected. This rule applies to any condition. There may be people that aren't good about keeping up their hygiene. This should not be the issue. Thus, it should not come up in conversation.
4. Stay away from 'steering'. Steering is considered a form of discrimination. A person may mention they have children. If there are vacant apartments near the property playground and vacant apartments throughout the property, show them apartments in these areas and let them decide.
5. Do not answer questions dealing with crime rate, etc. Again, these questions could pose a problem with the regulatory agencies.
6. Entreat all applicants with the same respect and demeanor. Get in the habit of presenting the same sales pitch to everyone.
7. Decide which apartments you will show and show only those until they are rented. Do not show a different apartment to different applicants. This could be misunderstood as discrimination or steering.
8. Watch how applicants are referred to when discussing information with management

Laws, Regulation, and Regulatory Agencies

personnel. Referring to a resident according to their ethnic background can be viewed as an act of discrimination.
9. Ensure all employees entreat the residents in the same manner. Do not allow 'favors' for some residents and not all.
10. Do not enter an apartment without giving prior 24 hours' notice to the resident. Make certain everyone on staff obeys the regulations of the contract as well as the resident.

These are just a few of the issues the regulatory agencies will look at and the first six rules will be attended to when a property is shopped. These issues are further discussed later in this book. In short everyone should always be professional and pleasant.

Competition

A property manager should always know the competition in the area. If there is a larger vacancy than usual and the manager wants to run apartment specials, then its best that those specials are competitive with the surrounding properties. One way to know the competition is to shop them. Most properties will give you rental information and what their occupancy rate is if asked, but how the competing property do business is where shopping them comes in.

Shopping competitive properties can create growth in the leasing consulting staff as well as the manager. A manager in one of our meetings stated he shopped this one competitor and was more enthused to rent an apartment from them than his own community. They showed such enthusiasm and interest in him from the time he entered their office until the time of his departure. He almost hated to leave. This encouraged him to improve his own presentations when they had prospective renters visit his property. Don't limit your information gathering to the telephone, go out and shop around!

Waiting Lists

It is most common to have a waiting list. Most properties depend on their waiting lists to fill vacancies as soon as they come available. But, on occasion, the waiting list may not prove efficient if not maintained. Maintaining a waiting list entails checking on the applications periodically. If an applicant hasn't been heard from in 30 to 60 days, then most likely they have found an apartment. Call the applicant at least every 30 days to see if there is still an interest in an available apartment.

There was a situation where an applicant had to move into an apartment before we could offer them one on our property. They called to inform us of their move and all their new information. When an apartment came available, we called to notify the applicant and scheduled when they would be available to move in.

Sometimes, an applicant cannot move within the allotted 1 to 2-week period. If the property has scheduled move-outs, then arrangements should be made around those move-outs. No apartment should be held more than 2 weeks for a move-in. Everyday an apartment is vacant costs the property money. These vacancy costs are referred to as losses to income. So, it's very important to have the vacancy filled as soon as possible.

The result of poor communication with the applicants of a waiting list is a ineffective waiting list. So, it is imperative that the leasing consultant keeps in contact with all the participants of the waiting list.

Apartment Availability

Apartment availability was touched on in the previous section. If there is no available apartment, then the applicant should be retained on a waiting list. If the waiting list is too large, then a schedule of when it will open again should be offered to the potential renter.

When notice of apartment availability is given, the leasing consultant should begin looking for a potential renter. The apartment should not be vacant for more than 2 weeks. The applicant should move in within 3 to 5 days after the apartment comes available if the apartment was in good to excellent condition. An apartment in good to excellent condition should take only 3 to 5 days to prepare with paint and carpet cleaning.

However, if major maintenance is required to prepare the apartment for occupancy, then there should be no more than a 1 to 2-week preparation period. If it takes more time, then the Accounting Executive should be notified because then the replacement and reserve accounts may be affected. In which case, extra monies not budgeted would be spent for possible carpet replacement, major wall repairs, fixture replacements, etc.

Overall, the leasing consultant is the most important person in retaining a prospective renter and scheduling a timely occupancy of the available apartment.

Last, it is important that the manager and the maintenance technician walk the apartment at the time of vacancy to get an idea of its availability and repairs. After the apartment has been prepared for move-in, the manager should walk the apartment once more with the maintenance technician to ensure that there are not any last-minute repairs required which may have been missed. Shortly, before the prospective renter comes in the sign the contract, the rental consultant should walk the apartment and walk the apartment, again with the renter before the contract is signed. In short, there should not be any 'surprises' awaiting the resident when at the time of move-in.

Leasing Up a Property

Property Lease ups can be a very time consuming and stressful job. During construction buildings come available one or sometimes two at a time. In most cases, a new property won't have very good roads and grass. Sometimes boards maybe the only sidewalks at the time the buildings come available for occupancy. In any wise, it's imperative that the new residents are notified of the conditions into which they are moving so that they are prepared to walk the boards and expect the dirt areas where grass will eventually be laid.

During the construction of a building problems may arise that may postpone the move-in process. Thus, again, the move-in rule should be applied. There would allow enough time for the manager and the maintenance technician to walk and careful examine each apartment before moving in the resident. If any problems are spotted, the construction crew can correct them before they become disasters. If it is timelier to have the maintenance technician perform the repairs, then let the technician do the repairs. This would be a learning process for the technician in case of new hardware or technology.

Schedule each move-in allowing time for questions and to walk the apartment. If two days have to be taken to move in a building, then take the two days. Have your maintenance technicians and office staff check periodically to ensure the residents moving in have no unforeseen happen stances. Make sure signs warning the residents of the trip hazards are in place.

The same rules for leasing should be followed when processing applications during a lease up. Of course, it the property is a Tax Credit property, there is a limited amount of time to lease the apartments and sometimes deciding the qualifications of an applicant can be very lenient. In the long run, leniency could cost the property monies in court costs and skip outs. Most importantly, a 'least up' property should be treated with the same care and concern as an established property.

The Lease Agreement

The Lease agreement informs the new resident of the privileges and the regulations of the property. It is a binding contract between landlord and resident for the purpose of renting the apartment and its maintenance.

At the time of the new resident move in, the agent of the owner should go through the provisions of the lease to ensure all binding parties have an understanding of the rules and regulations outlined. The pages to follow will explain some of the clauses that most contracts or lease agreements will have listed.

Identifying Parties

Of course, every lease has to identify the lessee, who is the resident and the lessor, who is the landlord. The information reflected in this section is the new residents' address, city and state of the property, building number if available, all the authorized occupants, the term of the contract, amount of the monthly rent and the payment requirements, utilities included in the monthly rental amount, and the parties bound to the contract.

Rent and Late Fees

The lease will list the amount of rent that is paid and where the rental amount is mailed or if the resident can just drop it off somewhere on property. Usually a late fee of $20.00 to $25.00 is stated to help deter the resident from making any late payments beyond the allotted grace period. Grace periods can range from 3 to 5 days. Seldom will there be a grace period greater than 5 days unless the property is privately owned.

Terms of payment can also include in what form the rental payment can be accepted. Most properties will only accept check or money order. Cash payments are frowned upon because of the greater risk management would face with interoffice theft and robberies.

Utilities most commonly included within the monthly rental payments are water, sewer and trash removal, and heating gas. Again, seldom will a landlord include electricity and telephone usage. There are properties that will have an additional cost for sewer and trash removal and water, but these properties are few.

The Binding Parties

The parties bound to the terms of the lease are usually the new resident(s) and the property. Sometimes the name of the owner's company is bound, but in any wise, the acting manager is never named.

The Lease Agreement

This is done because managerial staffing changes and sometimes even managing companies change. In the property management industry, property owners seldom manage their own properties.

The trend has been to hire in management companies who specialize in the managing of rental properties of all sorts; from apartment buildings and complexes, to townhouse communities. These companies are well informed with the regulations regarding the renting of apartments and townhouses.

Resident Obligations

The lease should always list what the residents' obligations are while living in the rented apartment. The following are the most common listed in a lease:

1. The resident is required to pay monthly rental installments on or by the date indicated in the lease agreement. If pay is paid beyond the allotted grace period, additional charges will be added to the rental payment. Occasionally, mention is made of breach of the contractual agreement and possible termination can result by not being timely with monthly rental payments.
2. There are regulations, which prohibit unsafe and unsanitary living conditions within a rental community. Thus, a clause advising the resident to maintain the premise in a clean and sanitary

condition is included. If the resident fails to comply with this clause, government agencies can charge the landlord with fines, penalties, and costs for the violation especially if the landlord allows this behavior to continue within the community.
3. In the prevention of fire, electrical, or water hazards or damages, the lease will inform the resident of the landlord's or agents of the landlord's right to enter the rental unit for maintenance or repairs. Agents of the landlord can include outside contractors. In which case, usually a property maintenance technician accompanies the outside contractor for the contractor's interest.
4. Most of the regulations listed in the lease will include the use of the facilities and amenities the property has to offer. If there is a violation in the use of these amenities, the resident will be given a change to comply with the rules governing the use of these facilities. Failure to comply will relinquish the residents' right to use these facilities.
5. The consideration of other residents in areas of noise and daily activity is listed always. The one of the biggest problems in an apartment community is noise. People forget that walls are thin and not everyone works a nine to five job. If this clause is stressed during the move in, then this won't be a reoccurring problem. Remember, appeal to the residents' sense of morality and fairness.
6. Apartment alterations can be a problem if not addressed. The landlord must always be in charge of what alterations are allowed. Some communities

The Lease Agreement

will allow a change in lighting and window treatments. Older communities will even allow the resident to paint and change the flooring if the apartment hasn't been upgraded. Regardless, the resident should always be told to what extent the apartment could be altered.

7. Pets can be a problem is a resident isn't responsible for cleaning up after them. If the property allows dogs and cats, a pet deposit and a higher rent is usually charged to compensate the landlord in case carpet or outside areas are affected by the pet. Again, the landlord should outline the restrictions and expected responsibilities around owning a pet.

8. Installation of appliances, namely a washer and dryer. You'd be surprised how many communities contain washers and dryers in apartment units that are not zoned for them. It is imperative to inform the resident the importance of adhering to the design restrictions of the apartment unit. Overloading electrical and plumbing lines can cause serious problems later for the resident and the landlord.

9. Parking can be a problem in an apartment community. Make sure that if there are unspoken rules of the community, that the new resident understands them.

   For example, there may be two parking places directly in front of two adjacent apartments. The unspoken or unwritten rule of the community maybe to allow only those residents closest to the parking places access. Outside visitors should not occupy these parking places out of regard for the residents.

Appeal to the residents' sense of well-being and fair play and explain these community 'respects.

10. Subleasing is usually prohibited. Before a resident move into a community, management screens them to see if they qualify for the property. At most times, even a background check is obtained. If a resident sublease, a lot of the checks and balances have not been followed and a problem may arise causing the resident to lose the apartment unit.
11. Most apartment communities will not allow any kind of business to be done out of the apartment. This may present a problem for the surrounding neighbors because of traffic and possibly violation of the noise policy. It is vital that the unit is used for which it was acquired.

Checklists

A checklist is list of the apartment's features that is used to assess the condition of the apartment unit at the time the resident moves in. This list is important in that at the time the resident moves out, any damages or flaws in the apartment at the time of move in that couldn't be repaired, will not be charged to the resident.

Most management companies allot a seven-day period after move in for the resident to mark down the condition of the apartment unit. After the seven-day period, any damages that are not noted on the checklist will be charged to the resident. Sometimes if an apartment checklist made by management before the

The Lease Agreement

resident moves in is placed in the apartment unit file, the resident can be given more time to turn their checklist in.

The checklist will include the rooms, walls, lights, doors, floors, carpeting, fixtures, appliances, windows, and anything else that is included in the apartment. There will also me a section on the checklist where the resident can check the condition or make a brief note for each apartment feature.

Breach of Contract

There is always a clause that outlines what is considered a breach of contract and the consequences involved should a resident or management be in breach of contract. Dependent upon how well the property is doing, the results can be termination of the lease agreement or just a slap on the wrist. If the resident had proved to be very good for the property, then more likely the breach will be brought to the resident's attention and compliance be required. If the breach causes a hazard for the livability of the property or its residents; good resident or not, the lease is terminated.

Security Deposits

A security deposit is the down payment to the landlord in case of damages in rental payment or physical damages to property after the resident moves out. This monetary payment is usually equivalent to a month's rent or a lesser amount. It is deposited and secured in a banking security deposit account for the duration of the residents' stay. At the time the resident decides to move out, thirty days from the time the resident moves and after the assessment of the apartment damages is made, whatever is left from the security deposit is mailed to the ex-resident.

It is required by law that the resident submit in writing to the management office, a forwarding address within four days after moving out of the community. Failure to do so, forfeits the resident's security deposit.

Application Fee

The lease will also include whether any fees paid before moving in are refundable. This fee is used to cover the cost of the application process. Some properties include the application fee as part of the move in costs. Other properties keep this fee separate from the total move in fees and costs. In most cases, the application fee is not refundable

Notice of Damages

After the resident moves out of the community, the landlord walks the apartment to assess if there are any damages. If there are damages, a notice or SODA (Statement of Deposit Account) is sent itemizing the damages and how much of the security deposit will be used to cover those damages.

The Lease Agreement

This statement has to be sent to the ex-resident within 30 days after they have moved. Then the ex-resident has 7 days to notify management if there is a discrepancy in the statement regarding charges. Management will then look over everything again. If there is no change, further explanation has to be required of the ex-resident. If there is no proof that the ex-resident is not responsible for the charges, another notice with a copy of the SODA should be sent along with a check for the balance owed, if any, from the security deposit account.

Landlord's Obligations

The Landlord's obligations are outline in most lease agreements. These responsibilities are usually outlined as a result of the HUD and Fair Housing guidelines. The following obligations listed are the most common found in lease agreements:

1. The Landlord has to accept the rent paid by the resident without regard to whether additional charges are included.
2. All common areas (areas that are accessible to all the residents) must be fit for intended resident use.
3. Each apartment in the community has to be kept in reasonable repair according to the health and safety laws set forth by local, state, and federal housing laws.

4. The landlord must not be partial to any resident in the provision of services regardless of sex, race, age (unless in an elderly housing community) color, religion, marital status, national origin, familial status, or handicap.
5. A 30-day notice has to be sent to all residents at the time of any revisions to the original contract.
6. These changes to contract must comply with all federal, state, and local housing laws even if they are related to the protection of the physical, health, safety, or peaceful enjoyment of the resident and his/her guest.

Renewal

The landlord has the option of renewing the lease every year with revision to monthly rental payments if there is no breach of contract by the resident. If the resident happens to breach the lease agreement before its maturity, the landlord can accelerate the total amount of rent claimed for the remaining time of the lease agreement. However, the apartment cannot be rented during the time paid for by the previous resident as a result of the accelerated amount requested by the landlord and granted by the courts.

If the resident submits a 30-day notice to vacate before the lease is renewed, the resident should submit a change of address within 7 days after the resident moves. Then a Security Deposit of Accounts should be issued within 30 days along with payment after all outstanding charges are subtracted.

The Lease Agreement

Damage by Fire or Other Casualty

If the leased premises are damaged or rendered inhabitable by fire, storm, earthquake or any other casualty, then the term of the lease is automatically terminated, and the resident is not responsible for the remaining rents owed from the time of the casualty.

In the event the damage to the residency is partial and the premises is partly habitable, then the rent is abated (reduced) until the premises is in full repair.

If the resident is responsible for the damages to the premises, then the resident will be billed for all repairs related to the casualty. Should there be a problem with the resident paying for the damages, then payment can be demanded through court proceedings.

Subordination

In the event that the property mortgages change, the lease will remain in effect and the resident is still obligated to all the terms of the lease agreed upon before the company change. If the resident refuses to abide by the terms of the lease agreement, then the Landlord or the Landlord's successor, assignors, assignees, or legal representatives can terminate the lease agreement.

No Waiver

Late rent notices, lease violation notices or any other notices may be sent to the resident in the event the resident is in violation of the lease. On occasion, the manager may fall behind in the issuance of these reminders because of unforeseen problems that may arise during the month. At which time, the resident is still held by the terms of the contract without the manager making any attempts to collect rents or enforce the lease agreement.

Possession

When a resident moves into the community, possession of the premises is not handled over until the following conditions are met:

1. The resident and the Landlord must both sign the lease agreement;
2. The previous resident has vacated the premises and all unit preparations have been completed;
3. The resident has paid first month's rent, security deposit, nonrefundable application fee, and any other charges required prior to residency.

If the manager is unable to deliver possession of the premises to the resident moving in, then the Landlord isn't liable for any losses gained by the resident. However, the resident can give written notice of cancellation before possession is obtained.

If the resident doesn't cancel, then the agent or Landlord can offer an abatement of the rent under the lease for the period between the lease date and the actual time of possession. The abatement would fulfill any losses incurred by the resident as a result of the delay.

False Statements

This clause informs the resident that all information submitted at the time of application around family income and compositions are correct. If any information is incorrect it could contribute to the termination of the resident's lease and charges could result for the indiscretion.

Addendums

There are a number of addendums that cover areas such as environmental conditions, which restrict the storage, or use of flammable substances; a drug-free housing addendum which restricts the use or sell of illegal drugs by the resident or visitors of the resident within the apartment community; there is a smoke detectors addendum which restricts the resident from tapering with the smoke detectors and disabling them; and any other addendums that are relevant to the type of community.

Insurances

There are a number of clauses, which cover the resident's requirement for renters and health insurances. The property has insurances that cover any damages as a result of neglect by the agents or contractors of the management team and this insurance covers any structural damages, amenities that are damaged or any other property owned by the management company.

If the resident suffers damages as a result of neglect by the agents or the contractors of management, then the Landlord is required to cover those damages. In conclusion, it is good to have insurance to cover all personal possessions and all occupants of the household.

Conclusion

Conclusively, the lease is one important document that should be thoroughly explained and understood by all parties that are binding. All adult residents that are moving onto the premises should sign the lease. The rule of thumb is to make all adult residents obligated to the conditions of the lease agreement.

Resident Retention

Another important part of property management is resident retention. Resident retention consists of different methods used to ensure the satisfaction of residents with the apartment community in which they have chosen to live. Holiday programs and activities, good maintenance and preventative maintenance programs, good communication between management and the residents, moderate rent increases, enforcing of the rules and regulations of the community, and promotion of community unity.

Community Communication

The best way to make your residents feel a part of a community is to be informative about the status of events around the community. A community newsletter is the best source for continued communication. A newsletter should include information about the surrounding community as well as things happening on the property.

There was an occasion when one of my residents noticed a white van parked near the bus stop where our children catch the school bus. This bit of information was published in a flyer to alert the residents to the presence of this suspicious vehicle. As a result, the van left the property and didn't return.

The residents near and around the bus stop watched the children every morning getting on the school bus and every evening as they were dropped off. The neighbors to our children kept an eye out for any further suspicious activity. The residents were also informed that the local police department was notified of the white van.

This promoted a sense of community amongst the residents and a unity was formed around the safety of our children. From that point, neighbors talked more, and the residents communicated more with management about the different things that were going on around them.

When the residents know that the manager will address the problems they incur, they will be more willing to trust the manager with information concerning the well-being of the property. Everyone will be willing to work together for the good of the entire property and its residents.

There were little things like what to use to clean walls and stove pans that the residents seemed to appreciate. Then there was information about the repairs that were to take place around the property. The residents feel more confident to stay in a community they are familiar with. This property remained 98% to 100% occupied for 2 ½ years.

Good Maintenance and Preventative Maintenance

Flyers and newsletters keep the residents informed about the activities in and around the apartment community. Another feature to resident retention is good maintenance and preventative maintenance. When a work order is submitted, the maintenance technician should attend to the request within a 24-hour period. If materials are required, then the resident should be notified of the delay and if the repair is an inconvenience, then if at all possible management should try to compensate the resident in some way by providing a temporary solution to their discomfort or a discount on their rent.

If there is a grievance between the resident and the maintenance technician, this should not interfere with maintenance repairs. The resident should be notified that no communication is allowed with the technician during repairs and if there is a concern, the concern should be addressed to the manager. It would be a good practice to advise the maintenance technician that it would be to their good interest not to converse with the residents during business hours.

At the time preventative maintenance measures are scheduled, the residents should be notified a few days ahead if they are required to prepare the area in need of maintenance. For example, if furnace filters are scheduled to be changed and the furnace area is also used as a storage area, then a few days' notice should be given allowing the resident enough time to clear that area. If for whatever reason the area isn't cleared, then a violation notice should be submitted to that resident.

Equal Treatment

The hardest situation for a manager living on the property is staying partial. There were times when residents invited me to dinner and I had to decline. In accepting one dinner invitation, I would have had to accept any dinner invitation from the entire property. Equal treatment is a big plus in resident retention. If a resident knows that management will not show any partiality, then they are more inclined to accept reprimand for their violations and are more willing to stay in a community that will treat them fairly. In society, everyone wants to be treated fairly. Thus, it is the same in an apartment community.

Holiday Programs and Activities

An apartment community with a strong festive motivation is usually a community that will have many participants in whatever activities arise. Most apartment communities will participant in decorating competitions and property picnics. Holiday parties, bake sales, informational meetings, are other activities a community will participate in.

There was an occasion the apartment complex next door to us had a shooting. A child found the parents' gun and accidentally shot himself. This posed an opportunity for me to have a gun safety seminar for the children and their parents on the property. We invited the local police department to hold the seminar and the turnout was great. Throughout the year, we had a good turnout for our 'Stranger Danger' seminar and other informative events the local police department offered.

As calamities arose, seminars and social events became management's response. In the end, the residents were well informed and united in each cause. The property became a close-knit community.

Moderate Rent Increases

Throughout the year, the manager becomes knowledgeable about the financial status of the property. This information should be submitted with a recommendation as to how much of a rent increase the property is capable of handling without losing residents. If the rent is raised too high, then residents will start looking for more reasonable living conditions.

In my own opinion, an analysis should be done for each resident at the time of contract renewal to determine if the resident can handle a rent increase and if so, how much of an increase. If an across the board $20.00 increase can be handled by everyone then so be it. If only a fraction of the property can handle a $20.00

increase, then management should seek a lesser amount that the property as a whole can handle or wait another year before raising rents.

But of course, this decision of rent increases is left up to the accounting executive who will base the final decision on the rental activities of the previous year. So, the manager should be thorough when reporting your monthly income and delinquencies. It could cause the loss of a few good residents.

Community Unity

There were instances that community unity was addressed in the previous sections. In conclusion, management is the key to promoting community unity. Management can bring the community together using a single crusade or just planned activities. Information sharing is another method of unifying a community. Community unity is a condition, which happens through personal involvement and experiences.

Attitude and Property Management

The most important attribute a manager can possess is a good attitude. You can have the best property with good residents, but a bad attitude can bring a property to ruin. A good attitude will cause a manager to seize opportunities for improvement and advancement for the property; or allow disappointments to create morale problems. There will be times when only property goals, personal values, good hard work, and a good attitude are the only motivating factors.

What is a good attitude? You may ask. Outwardly, it is the way mood and disposition is displayed to others as a response to the way the world is viewed at that particular moment. Attitude is a mind-set; it is the mental outlook at things around us. Our perceptions of situations influence our attitudes; in which perception is the process we view and interpret our environment.

In most cases, negative situations are magnified, and positive situations are minimized. Instead, the negative situation should be diffused and the positive emphasized, this would be the first step in creating a positive mind-set. Whereas, attitude is actually an ongoing, dynamic, sensitive, perceptional process; viewing each element of circumstance as either an opportunity for improvement or growth.

Of course, it wouldn't be possible to keep a positive attitude at all times. In fact, there are situation that wouldn't merit a cheerful disposition. In which case, it would be prudent to be supportive and optimistic. Most problems have resolutions! Most tragedies can be tolerated and be accepted. In short, we must overcome and continue to stand.

There were times in my property management career the tasks of the day became overwhelming. But there were also times I realized getting a 'jump' on things meant arriving an hour or two early for work. A manager should arrive early for work allotting time to prioritize the agenda for the day and set out to complete at least the most important items listed. This can contribute to reinforcing a good attitude towards job responsibilities. A positive job perspective encourages the ability to address problems and take action to resolve them in a more effective way before they worsen.

The *High Expectancy Success Theory* states that the more success that is expected from a situation, the more successful the outcome will be. A rental consultant that has the attitude that more applications will be obtained for the day will more than likely succeed to bring in more applications. There is an attitude to work harder in encouraging and persuading the potential renter to apply for occupancy. There is usually a higher drive in pleasantries. But in the end, the task the rental consultant sets out to do will have some degree of success.

Attitude can enhance what is already prevalent. A person need not be beautiful to have a wonderful disposition. Hence, a not so handsome person can appear to be more beautiful just through the image of attitude projected. Then what role does attitude play in personality?

Personality is enhanced through the type of attitude a person projects. An optimistic person tends to draw more people. People will shun a pessimist. A highly motivated personality can transform a dull personality into an exciting one. The reason is positive traits seem to 'shine through' other personality characteristics projecting a brighter and more attractive total image to others.

Persons in sales seem to be highly motivated and project an enthusiastic attitude towards their products. If a property manager has confidence in the product, then that attitude will be projected upon the potential renter. They will have confidence in what the manager tells them concerning the unit to be rented and be just as excited about applying.

In the business community, people tend to depend more on their intellect and appearance not realizing the importance of attitude. They depend heavily on talent and forget that people enjoy being around cheerful and optimistic people. To be successful in business would mean to have an attitude to succeed in winning over the confidence of the client and projecting that success and confidence in our accounting executives, our maintenance and office personnel, and our own abilities to make our property successful.

Handling the 'Hostile' Resident

There's a biblical saying that goes like this, "A soft answer will turn away wrath, but speaking grievous words will stir up anger." I had been in many situations where I had to calm down an angry resident. I had been cursed out and even threatened, but all went well, anyway. I've heard of other managers being shot and killed, beaten, and their property vandalized. Fortunately, I had not been beaten or shot.

A caller called the office because the maintenance in their apartment wasn't done correctly. The problem reoccurred an hour after the technician left the apartment. I answered the phone and listened as the caller threatened to call the local newspaper about the poor service.

I waited until the resident was finished. My reply was, "I will let you talk to the maintenance supervisor about the problem, then I'll speak with you again after it's been taken care of." The call was passed on to the supervisor and he received the same complaint but this time the resident wasn't as hostile. The supervisor and the technician returned to the angry resident's apartment and repaired the problem. The technician just needed a little training in resolving that particular problem.

The phone rang, again. I answered it to find the same resident on the other line, but with a different demeanor. "I'd like to apologize for coming off on you like that," the caller said. "I know it wasn't your fault, but I want you to know I appreciate you for letting me vent my frustration out on you. I promise it won't happen, again." I felt so gratified to receive an apology from a once hostile resident and then to know I did something right.

A lot of times, being a human being and having pride can get in the way of handling a hostile situation. Years later, I was transferred to a larger complex. It had snowed, and a resident came in early that morning complaining of the snow that wasn't shoveled in front of his mother's apartment. It prevented her from going to work. He pounded my desk trying to intimidate me, demanding that it be taken care of immediately. Calmly I replied, "I'll check with the maintenance crew on the snow removal status and get back with you." This answer wasn't enough. Once more he yelled and pounded on my desk demanding that it be taken care of NOW. Then he stormed out of the office and slammed the door behind him.

The cleaning people came in shortly after and asked, "Who was that acting like that?"

I laughed and explained what had happened. Then, I radioed the maintenance technicians to see when they would be shoveling the building where the complaining resident lived with his mother.

Later, that week, the man called back and thanked me for getting the job done. He realized he was out of line and although he didn't directly apologize, it was heard in his voice and demeanor.

Sometimes just listening and allowing a resident to vent their angry can help more than 'demanding your respect!' When a situation has cooled down, then a conversation concerning respect can be discussed.

"She smeared dog mess on my front door!" the maintenance technician complained.

"I told your son not to let your dog mess in my flowers and he purposely let him. When I told your wife, nothing was done. So, I did something!" the woman replied, angrily. Then she turned to the manager. "You'd better do something about this!"

"Yeah! She'll do something about this! You're off the property!" the maintenance technician yelled.

The manager waited a moment until the technician and the resident were done yelling. Then, she asked her technician to leave while she talked to the resident. He left.

"You know you're in violation of your contract, don't you?"

"I don't care, he was wrong!" she replied.

"And you were right?"

The woman lowered her head, a little.

"You smeared poop on my door. That door belongs to the property, not my tech. You violated your contract and the contract says I have to terminate your lease for something like this," the manager scolded.

"Well, I did go back and clean it off the door," the woman said in a calmer voice.

"Well, that's good to know," the manager replied, then thought a moment. "What I'll do is write this up and place it in your file as a slap on the wrist. In turn, you will have to write a letter explaining what happened and how you went back to clean the door. Have a neighbor who witnessed the situation write a letter as a witness."

'Thanks!"

"I'll talk with my tech about the dog! Just don't put me in this position again. I wouldn't want to have to terminate your contract. Okay?"

"Thanks, again. I'll take care of that first thing," she replied then left.

These situations actually happened in the detail that they happened. Unbelievable! You might say, but learning the moods of people and their personalities can help in the long run. This lady had a temper and I knew how she felt and what made her 'tick' because I had the same bad temper. I would have done the same thing. So, I looked at the situation from her point of view, and then let her see our position on this situation.

I didn't demand my respect because I already had their respect under normal circumstances. I had the upper hand in all situations that confirmed a violation of contract. Why push around the weight everyone knew I had. I waited until the resident blew off steam, then I handled the situation. No self-respect was bruised. I did my job.

When dealing with a hostile resident, remember these three things:

1. Don't take it personal! The resident is complaining about the job, not the person. They may make references to you as a person, but remember after the problem is resolved; they have short-changed themselves.
2. Let the resident blow off steam! Sometimes if a problem is ongoing and it seems to them it will never be resolved, it makes them angry. Put yourself in their place. Listen with a sympathetic ear, then show the resident you're there to help.
3. Do your job! Stay job orientated. The lease agreement gives you the power over your property. You are the 'king or queen' of your realm. Use that power to resolve the problems at hand. When the situation is calmed down, then state the importance of the resident showing correct behavior and assure the resident their problem will be resolve.

Property management is a career and shouldn't interfere with your peace of mind. When a heated situation cools down then read the riot act to the resident that was out of hand. Trying to put out a fire with gasoline will cause a much bigger problem. Remember stick with the contract!

Choosing the 'Right' Employees

Frankly, I don't think there are credentials that will indicate you are interviewing the right person for the job. Or a set number of rules that will tell you, this person is the one. All I would be able to offer is my own experiences. I feel a good candidate for a job in property management has to be enthusiastic about the job. Someone who is ready for a challenge and wants to see that challenge met.

When I interviewed for my maintenance technician, I looked for the following traits:

1. Enthusiasm; the technician or office assistant has to be excited about things coming together. Work can be enjoyable if a result is expected. A technician should be excited about getting a 100% completion on his unit. If the technician strives to achieve a no repairs required status on his completed unit, it's a challenge that was accomplished.
2. Professionalism; the interviewee has to have some type of 'by the book' attitude or background. If so, then little will be in doubt about whether the job is done or is being done

3. according to procedure. These people will know to follow protocol in referring residents and in addressing situations according to their job requirements.
4. Experience; No all interviewees will have the experience required, but a working knowledge and a little experience should at least be acceptable. You can always build on a foundation. Most managers would prefer someone who has a minimum amount of experience for that very reason.
5. Personal Appeal; A personality can go a long way when dealing with people. I worked with one technician that seemed to swoon the most vicious people. He was the most likeable person I knew. If no one else could gain entry into a resident's apartment, he could. When an angry resident saw this technician, they would calm down and be smiling by the end of his conversation. This guy was very handy to the property manager we worked with.
6. Team Orientated; No man's an island. There are jobs that require the effort of the whole management staff to complete. Everyone working together helps reduce the stress factor for everyone. If the technician postpones work orders, the office assistant and the manager suffer with hearing angry residents. Sometimes, the technician will suffer with the ordeal. If the office staff doesn't correctly write up the work order, the technician has to

Choosing the 'Right' Employees

wrestle with what needed to be done. Teamwork is a must.

7. Assertive; When things arise that need immediate attention and an employee has the ability to perform that task, there should not be any question in the tasks resolution. There were times I couldn't get my accounting executive on immediate decisions I needed, so I had to take the initiative and make the right decision. I notified my accounting executive later. Sometimes I'd make the right choices and other times not so right a choice. But I learned as I went along.

8. Dedicated; There has to be some degree of dedication to the profession. I had a technician that was so dedicated to the property that he walked the property every night checking the porch lights of every apartment. If one was out, he would replace them before the resident had a change to put in a work order.

9. Commonsense; Commonsense dictates that if there is trash lying about on the grounds and it's been laying there for a few days, then the manager would know you're not doing your job. Or if trash is outside the dumpsters, then you're not being attentive to the dumpsters. Managers want to know that their employees are at least trying to do a very good job and will do what needs to be done without being told the majority of their employment.

10. Ethics; An employee with good work ethics will always ensure that the job is completed before the end of the day. The company's time is well spent, and no time is wasted doing things that are not job related. The employee will be to work minutes earlier to have that cup of coffee or be on time to work. The maintenance technician I had would do grounds on the way to work and still get to work in time to make coffee for me and we would go over what the agenda was for the day, sipping coffee; all before working time.
11. Motivated; A motivated employee will always find new ways of doing things and improving things. One maintenance technician could find a part for a repair. Later, we found out the part we would have to order would take a few days to arrive. So, the technician created a makeshift part for the repair until the actual part came in. I think this guy was more impressed with himself than I was with him.

Realistically, you might not find anyone who possesses all those quality, because they are rare to find. But if you find people you at least have good work ethics, motivated, and team orientated, then you've got a winning employee. I think these are the most important and can lead to developing the other traits listed above.

A good management team can cause the property to run like a well-oiled machine. A well-trained management team can cause the property to be a

Choosing the 'Right' Employees

pleasant place to work and to live. The manager's job is made easier when everyone knows what to do and how to do it. Last, a good staff has the motivation to do their best.

Managing Stress

The definition of stress is an unpleasant state of emotional and physiological arousal that people experience in situations that they perceive as dangerous or threatening to their well-being. Stress can mean different things to different people. To some people, stress can mean events or situations that make them feel tension, pressure, or negative emotions such as anxiety and anger.

In property management, there are situations that can bring on those emotions. But, again, don't take them personal. Much of the stress in our lives comes from our jobs, personal relationships, and everyday living circumstances. We handle them every day.

As property management personnel, we deal with driving to work or living on property. These promote stress. We deal with working with unpleasant contractors or dealing with resident concerns which can be stressful. When someone isn't performing their job, this can cause problems that will result in stress. In any wise, here is information that should be considered about stress.

The Effects of Stress

When a person is stressed out, they will display anxious thoughts and difficulty concentrating or remembering. Outward behaviors will change; teeth clenching, hand wringing, pacing, nail biting, and heavy breathing are typical outward signs of stress. Anxiety is an off-set of stress; butterflies in the stomach, cold hands and feet, dry mouth, and increased heart rate are all symptoms.

A Stress Response

When a person realizes a situation is stressful, the body responses by heightened physiological and emotional arousal. The nervous system is activated which prepares the body for action by directing the adrenal glands to secrete excessive amounts of adrenaline and norepinephrine. As a result, the heart beats more rapidly, muscle tension increases, blood pressure rises, and blood flow is diverted from our internal organs and skin to our brain and muscles. This reaction is referred to as the 'fight-or-flight response. At this point the body is energized to either confront the threat or flee from it.

Another stress response involves the hypothalamus and the pituitary gland; these are the important parts of the brain that regulate hormones and bodily functions. During times of stress, the hypothalamus directs the pituitary gland to secrete adrenocorticotropic hormone. This hormone stimulates the outer layer, or cortex, of the adrenal glands to release glucocorticoids, which is the stress hormone cortisol.

A Canadian scientist, Hans Selye noticed that patients with different illnesses shared many of the same symptoms, such as muscle weakness, weight loss, and apathy. He believed these symptoms were a result of the body's reaction to stress. In 1960, he did studies using rats that proved this point. When he exposed these rats to a variety of physical 'stressors', they all come up with the same symptoms; enlargement of the adrenal glands, shrinkage of the thymus gland (it regulates the immune system), and bleeding stomach ulcers.

Selye introduced a three-stage model of the stress response that he termed the General Adaptation Syndrome. The first of the three-stages was alarm. This is where the body is alerted of the stressor. The second stage is the resistance stage. Here is where the body adapts to the stressor and continues to resist it with a high physiological arousal level. The last stage is exhaustion; the body is vulnerable to disease and possibly death.

You see why I decided to put this section in this book. I experienced a great amount of stress when I worked the property management profession. But because I did not know how to deal with stress, I started to get sick and I experienced fatigue. My boss tried transferring me to a less stressful position and property, but until I learned to shut myself down, it didn't help. Finally, I had to quit and choose another profession. Preferably this one because writing relaxes me.

Mental Illness

Not only is physical health affected by stress but count mental health, also. People who experience long periods of stress and deal poorly with it may become irritable, socially withdrawn, and emotionally unstable. Difficulty concentrating and solving problems are also symptoms of mental stress.

Years before I worked property management, I worked in a large well-known firm in the computer operations department. Down the hall was the accounting department. I knew this wonderful person that I thought had it together. One day we were leaving when this woman started crying hysterically. She had so much stress, it caused her to breakdown. I'll tell you, this was a scary thing to me. I thought this woman was hard as nails, but even she could not handle the stress in her department.

Some people who are under a lot of tension and stress can start off suffering from extreme anxiety, depression, or other severe emotional problems. But, in the end they may end up breaking down nothing is done to relieve that stress.

Coping with Stress

There are two types of coping strategies: problem-focused coping and emotion-focused coping. The goal of both these strategies is to control one's stress level. In problem-focused coping, a person takes action to modify, avoid, or minimize the threatening situation. This helps to alleviate the negative emotions surrounding stress. In emotion-focused coping, people deal with their emotions around the situation. They rethink a situation in a more positive light, try to relax, go into denial, or have wishful thinking.

Out of the two coping strategies, Selye chose the problem-focused method to be the most effective. I tend to agree.

In property management, manages must always find new ways to resolve problems and approach them head on. Having a good supportive staff helps.

Social Support

When a person has the support of their fellow workers, family, and friends, it helps to relieve stress. There were times when a resident would come in and compliment me on how well the property was kept. This made me feel the job was worthy working. Then there were days that the support of my staff helped me through bitter times with residents.

Social support systems provide emotional sustenance, tangible resources and aid, and information we need. Having a support system makes one feel cared about and valued. I felt great when my accounting executive would visit my property. Also, she would point out the things I lacked in doing a better job, just knowing what I needed to work on relieved a lot of the stress I felt on my job. Occasionally, she would even call just to tell me how good a job I was doing.

Did you know that research linked social support to good health and superior ability to cope with stress? Well it did. Research suggested that even the perception of social support can help people cope with stress. Remember the body reacts to stress adversely and can cause medical problems both physically and mentally. So, if you can be sincerely supportive of your associate, pretend you are!

Relaxation

There is life after property management. It's important to include relaxation into your daily routine. After work, do aerobics; walking, running, biking, or skiing. These activities will keep your stress levels down. If you're not an athletic person, meditate or listen to music. Do something that will relax you and take your mind off the job. Like I said, writing was my relaxation tool. The only way I could successfully reduce stress in my life was change professions and do what relaxes me – write!

Managing Stress

Do misunderstand me, I loved property management, or I would not be doing this book. Any career you choose should be a pleasure to do or you shouldn't do it. But, in any wise, it would be good to leave work at work and go home to relax.

I cared about my job in property management to the point of obsession. I had to know what was going on at all time on my property. I couldn't go home and be home. I had to call the property. At one point, I took the property phone home with me. I lived next door to the office, so the cordless worked at my house. And don't think the residents didn't take advantage of that opportunity. They did! Residents are the most impatient people you want to deal with. Sometimes they can wait until working hours to see the manager. If you live on site, watch out!

Handling Emergencies

I decided to put this section after the handling stress section and you'll know why. Sometimes emergencies will arise on a property and a new manager should know what to do in case of one of those emergencies.

Apartment Flooding

Bang! Bang! Bang! The manager was awakened by the hard knocks at the front door. She slowly got out of bed and finally reached the door. She peered out to see a resident. It was 2:30 am in the morning. She opened the door, and took a good look. She couldn't believe her eyes.

"What happened to you?" the manager asked.

Standing before her was a small framed Caucasian woman soaked with water from head to toe. "I was dreaming I was in Hawaii under a water fall. When I woke up, I was really under a waterfall." The lady replied.

"Oh my God!" the manager looked over the woman's shoulder to see a fire truck, police cars and crowd of residents standing around one of the apartment buildings.

"They need you to open the door to the apartment over me," the woman finally informed her.

The manager dashed out and pushed through the crowd to where the police and fire marshal stood waiting. She fumbled for the right key then opened the door to the upstairs garden style apartment. Water gushed out around everyone's ankles. It was unbelievable.

"Oh my God!" the police officer exclaimed. "It looks like a river flowing down those stairs."

The manager and one of the officers pulled themselves up the stairs into the apartment to see where the water was coming from. They made their way to the second bathroom where the angle stops behind the toilet had come loose. Suddenly, the water started to die down.

"We shut off the water to the building," the fire marshal yelled up the stairs.

"Great!" the manager replied. The manager walked over to the closet where the water shutoff valve was to the apartment. Then, the policeman and the manager started down the stair out the apartment.

This situation really happened in the detail that was expressed above. The woman ended up in a hotel that the complex paid for and then moved into another unit a few days later. At the time, the property was still

Handling Emergencies

under construction, so the Construction Company was responsible for repairs to the building, the vacant apartments, and the occupied apartments. Fortunately, only one occupied apartment suffered major damage. The other apartments needed minor repairs and were still livable.

In case of a flood, shut down the water to the apartment and check the apartment for damages. Let the maintenance technicians repair the damages and do the plumbing. If they do not have plumbing experience, notify your accounting executive, then call in a plumber. Please note that you should always notify your accounting executive of the emergency and the status of its resolution.

Fire

At the time of fire, the resident or the neighboring residents should have already called the fire trucks. Notify the accounting executive of what is happening. Make sure all the residents are out of the building and are accounted for. After the fire is put out, try to find out what happened. If the surrounding apartments are not livable, the complex should put the residents up for the night at a hotel. It would be in the best interest of the complex if management starts an account with a local hotel for such occasions.

Find out as much details as possible about the fire and make out an incident report. A copy should be sent to the accounting executive and the main office who will in turn send this information to the insurance company. Make sure the technician takes pictures of the damages and check into pricing for repairs. This is information the insurance company and the Management Company will need.

If the damage is a result of resident negligence or an unforeseen accident, then the resident's renter's insurance company should be contacted. If the fire's a result of management's negligence, then matter should be handled according to contract and law. In any wise, the accounting executive should be consulted for procedures dealing with these types of emergencies.

Incident Reports

It is important to always fill out an incident report for any happenstance that may occur on the property. The incident report can be used to recall important conditions around the mishap in case a resident wants to involve the count system.

Incident reports should also include pictures and documented statements from witnesses if required. There should be a copy kept by the manager and a copy sent to the Management Company and accounting executive.

The reports should be filled out for the following: slip and falls, fires, floods, sewer backups, any damage to company property or resident property, trip-hazard situations, and anything that may involve the property.

Handling Emergencies

It is a must to complete this report within a timely manner, preferably within 48 hours from the incident.

www.ingramcontent.com/pod-product-compliance
Lightning Source LLC
Chambersburg PA
CBHW022019170526
45157CB00003B/1286